DAY BY DAY

THE RHYTHM OF THE BIBLE IN THE BOOK OF COMMON PRAYER

BY BENJAMIN SARGENT

The Latimer Trust

Day by Day: The Rhythm of the Bible in the Book of Common Prayer ©
Benjamin Sargent 2012

ISBN 978-1-906327-11-8

Cover photo: Ear of wheat on the background of the rising sun © joda –
Fotolia.com

Bible translations are author's own.

BWHEBB, BWHEBL, BWTRANSH [Hebrew]; BWGRKL, BWGRKN, and
BWGRKI [Greek] Postscript® Type 1 and TrueTypeT fonts Copyright ©
1994-2011 BibleWorks, LLC. All rights reserved. These Biblical Greek and
Hebrew fonts are used with permission and are from BibleWorks
(www.bibleworks.com).

Published by the Latimer Trust July 2012

The Latimer Trust (formerly Latimer House, Oxford) is a conservative
Evangelical research organisation within the Church of England, whose
main aim is to promote the history and theology of Anglicanism as
understood by those in the Reformed tradition. Interested readers are
welcome to consult its website for further details of its many activities.

The Latimer Trust
c/o Oak Hill College
London N14 4PS UK
Registered Charity: 1084337
Company Number: 4104465
Web: www.latimertrust.org
E-mail: administrator@latimertrust.org

Foreword to the Anglican Foundations Series

The recent celebration of the 350th anniversary of the 1662 *Book of Common Prayer* has helped to stimulate a renewed interest in its teaching and fundamental contribution to Anglican identity. Archbishop Cranmer and others involved in the English Reformation knew well that the content and shape of the services set out in the Prayer Book were vital ways of teaching congregations biblical truth and the principles of the Christian gospel. This basic idea of '*lex orandi, lex credendi*' is extremely important. For good or ill, the content and shape of our meetings as Christians is highly influential in shaping our practice in following the Lord Jesus Christ.

Furthermore, increased interest in the historic formularies of the Church of England has been generated by the current painful divisions within the Anglican Communion which inevitably highlight the matter of Anglican identity. In the end our Anglican Foundations cannot be avoided since our identity as Anglicans is intimately related to the question of Christian identity, and Christian identity cannot avoid questions of Christian understanding and belief. While the 39 Articles often become the focus of discussions about Christian and Anglican belief (and have been addressed in this series through *The Faith We Confess* by Gerald Bray) the fact that the 1662 *Book of Common Prayer* and the Ordinal are also part of the doctrinal foundations of the Church of England is often neglected.

Thus the aim of this series of booklets which focus on the Formularies of the Church of England and the elements of the different services within the Prayer Book is to highlight what those services teach about the Christian faith and to demonstrate how they are also designed to shape the practice of that faith. As well as providing an account of the origins of the Prayer Book services, these booklets are designed to offer practical guidance on how such services may be used in Christian ministry nowadays.

It is not necessary to use the exact 1662 services in order to be true to our Anglican heritage, identity and formularies. However if we grasp the principles of Cranmer which underpinned those services then modern versions of them can fulfil the same task of teaching congregations how to live as Christians which Cranmer intended. If we are ignorant of the principles of Cranmer then our Sunday gatherings will inevitably teach something to Anglican congregations, but it will not be the robust biblical faith which Cranmer promoted.

So our hope is that through this Anglican Foundations series our identity as Anglicans will be clarified and that there will be by God's grace a renewal of the teaching and practice of the Christian faith through the services of the Church of England and elsewhere within the Anglican Communion.

Mark Burkill and Gerald Bray

Series Editors, The Latimer Trust

CONTENTS

1.   Preface

At the beginning of this short study, I'd like to say something of what the *Book of Common Prayer* means to me personally as well as how I am approaching it here. I became a Christian as a teenager after being persuaded that the resurrection of Jesus Christ was an historical fact which demanded that I take the Lord Jesus and his claims seriously. My early knowledge of what God had done for me through Christ was somewhat sketchy, as was my understanding of what it meant to be a Christian. On both of these, I am sure I have much still to learn as I see more of glory of the cross and learn more of the difficult lessons of discipleship. However, the *Book of Common Prayer* was invaluable in my early growth as a Christian. Using the daily offices, I absorbed a great deal of Scripture and grew in my understanding of the vileness of my sin and the scope of God's mercy. By reading and investigating the Articles of Religion I grasped more fully the great doctrines of how my salvation was achieved and saw something pragmatic and realistic about what it meant to be a follower of the Lord Jesus. Perhaps naïvely, I was delighted by the idea of belonging to a Church which owned such a clear and biblical definition of faith as the Articles, as well as such a powerful and biblical liturgy. Today, as a clergyman, I am fortunate enough to serve a Church in which the Prayer Book plays a significant role, with Matins as a principal service most Sundays. However, the focus of my academic research and publication has been New Testament studies, with a secondary interest in contemporary philosophical theology. So I apologize in advance if this study reflects these interests too much but pray that it brings glory to God alone as it helps us to explore what it means to be a faithful Christian of the Anglican Church.

2.   Introduction

2.1   *Anglican Identity and the Past*

Christian identity is always conceived of through some relation to the past. It is the historical reality of Jesus of Nazareth, his deeds, his death, his resurrection and his exaltation, which define us as his disciples. Hence, every difficult situation and decision of the Christian life involves some questioning of this historical reality: 'what would Jesus say, think or have me do?' 'How should I approach difficult decisions in life, knowing that I have a heavenly inheritance to live for, made possible through the death and resurrection of the Lord Jesus?' And yet the New Testament writers affirm the importance of finding our identity as disciples, not simply in that one historical reality (though it is of course preeminent), but also as part of an historical people of God. This is especially important in the Theology of the Epistle to the Hebrews. In Hebrews chapter 11, the readers of the epistle are shown an astonishing display of God's people of the past whose deeds offer examples of the faithfulness to which the author urges the readers.[1] These great witnesses of the past are said to surround readers, the would-be witnesses of the present, defining what faithfulness ought to look like in concrete terms. Likewise, in Hebrews 3:6, readers are spurred on to remain in the household of God, served by Moses in the past, as they continue to

---

[1]   This call to faithfulness, to continue in the profession of Christ, is seen Hebrews 2:1, 3:6, 3:12,4:1-3, 4:14, 6:4-6 etc. On the relation of the past to the identity present see Guy G. Stroumsa, 'The Christian Hermeneutical Revolution and its Double Helix' in *The Uses of Sacred Books in the Ancient World*, T. Baarda, A. van der Kooij and A. S. van der Woude (ed.) (Leuven: Peiters. 1998) p 13 argues that the hermeneutical 'revolution' in which the past is joined to the present is due to a reassessment of 'belatedness', a community's distant position in time from aetiological events, that enables the present to be seen as an authoritative extension of the past. Cf. Paul Ellingworth, 'Jesus and the Universe in Hebrews,' *Evangelical Quarterly* 58:4. 1986. p 349.

hold fast to the hope of the Gospel.[2] The notion of informing present identity through reference to the past of which contemporary Christians are seen to be a part, can also be found in 1 Peter. For instance, in 1 Peter 3:5-6 the godly women of Israel's past (and Sarah in particular) are held up as an example to Peter's Christian readers or hearers. Sarah's example comes with the promise of becoming her children if such people 'do good and do not stop once through fear'. God's people of the present (the readers of 1 Peter) learn what it is to be God's people by considering the example of Sarah, one of God's people of the past. Yet this is not something only found in the New Testament. The idea of the people of the present understanding their identity through the people of the past and, consequently, the process by which they came to be who and where they are, is illustrated well by the 'confession' of Deuteronomy 26:5-10.[3]

> A wandering Aramaean was my Father, and he went down to Egypt and sojourned there with a small people. And it was that they became a great nation, strong and numerous. But the Egyptians treated us wickedly and caused us to be afflicted, giving us to hard labour. And we cried out to YHWH, the God of our Fathers, and YHWH heard our voice and saw our suffering, our work and our oppression. So YHWH brought us out of Egypt with a mighty hand and an outstretched arm, with great fear and signs and wonders. He brought us to this place and gave us this land, a land flowing

---

[2] See also Hebrews 3:7-4:11. Stephen Motyer, 'The Psalm Quotations of Hebrews 1: A Hermeneutic-Free Zone?' *Tyndale Bulletin* 50:1. 1999, p 8 writes that '...historical distance is by no means collapsed in [the] use of the Old Testament. In fact, a sense of historical progression from the Exodus, to the settlement in the land, to the kingship and to the present is fundamental to the treatment of Psalm 95 and 'the rest' in Hebrews 3-4.'

[3] The term 'confession', in the sense of a liturgical confession of faith, rather than a confession of sin, is used by Samuel Rolles Driver, *A Critical and Exegetical Commentary on Deuteronomy* (Edinburgh: T & T Clark. 1895), p 288. Cf. G. Braulik, 'Wie aus Erzählung ein Bekenntnis wird; das Credo Israels – Eine Kurzformel des Glaubens', *Entschluss* 38. 1983. pp 24-26. Gerhard von Rad, *Deuteronomy: A Commentary* (London: SCM. 1966), pp 158-159 notes that this confession lacks any mention of the Sinai Covenant, despite the importance that event assumes in Deuteronomy. He suggests that the confession may therefore reflect some much older material than Deuteronomy itself, since it is unlikely to be composed by the Deuteronomist or a Deuteronomistic school.

with milk and honey. And now I bring the firstfruits of the soil that you, YHWH, have given me.

What is interesting here is the move from describing history in the third person to description in the first person. Those who are asked to use this confession of faith are to see themselves in the suffering people of God in Egypt. This is astonishing, given that Deuteronomy itself makes it quite clear that those who suffered in Egypt are not those who stand on the brink of entering into the land promised to them.[4]

It is certainly true that from the earliest testimony, the people of God have sought to understand their identity in relation to the lives of godly exemplars in previous generations of God's people. The task of articulating what it means to be a Christian is to be undertaken with some consciousness of where contemporary Christians have come from in terms of an historical process. The series of which this booklet is a part rightly makes the assumption that the practice and beliefs of earlier generations of Christians within the Church of England, embodied in the *Book of Common Prayer*, is worthy of serious discussion and study in relation to the question of contemporary Anglican Identity. It will be argued that the *Book of Common Prayer* has much to contribute to this question. Yet the relation of the *Book of Common Prayer* to contemporary Anglican identity is not as simple as many suggest. The *Book of Common Prayer* should not be seen to embody some sort of pristine Christianity, the use of which must be resumed wherever it has disappeared. It is not as though the language of the *Book of Common Prayer* is better than all other forms of the English language at both expressing the truths of God and addressing him reverently, though it

---

[4] Deuteronomy 2:14-18. This is seen also in Psalm 95:11 in which God urges people at a later date to heed his voice, lest they become like the wilderness generation who failed to enter into the land as God's rest.

does both of these well.[5] I would like to see the *Book of Common Prayer* better known by Christians today. I would like to see more liturgy in the Church of England produced to the same high standard and theological clarity as the Prayer Book. I would like to know that future generations will have the opportunity to see the majesty of God's grace through the *Book of Common Prayer* in which it is wonderfully expressed. But I do not think it necessary to give the Prayer Book centre stage in the worship of the local Church, indeed, in many places, to do so would be a retrograde step away from practice which reflects that of the primitive Church which Cranmer

---

[5] The commonly expressed notion that the language of the *Book of Common Prayer* is appropriately 'theological' or 'reverent' English is pure nonsense. This can be seen, for example in the otherwise helpful article by Ian Robinson, '"And Life is Growth": The Development of the Prayer Book', *Faith and Worship* 57, 2004, who writes about the 'hostility to religious style from the 1960s onwards' (p 20) and writes that 'one of the most serious disservices of the new liturgies of the last half century has been to put a stopper on the native tradition of religious English' (p 17). In what sense can traditional language be described so exclusively as 'religious English' or 'religious style'? The Holy Scriptures themselves abound with common and contemporary language. The people of Israel were apparently happy to include Aramaic texts such as Daniel within their Hebrew 'canon' and the New Testament writers clearly had no qualms about expressing the most glorious dealing of God with his fallen creatures through the medium of Koine Greek, the language of the merchants. Not only did they use this 'common' form of Greek, in many cases they used it with little reference to grammatical norms. In fact, the clearest attestation of an archaizing tendency from the period is the use of cuneiform script in some of the Qumran scrolls, such as 11QPs[a] for the word YHWH. The Qumran community are well known for their sectarian exclusivity and consequent failure to engage with broader society. The danger of upholding a particular form of archaic language as the proper means of addressing God reverently is that Christian discourse about the God of love, like Qumranic discourse about the Teacher of Righteousness and the Man of Lies etc., becomes a symptom of a broader disengagement with the society to which we, as Christians, wish to speak. I believe something similar to this is argued by Paul Griffin, 'Necessary or Expedient', *Faith and Worship* 68. 2011. pp 46-48. Cf. Stella Brook, *The Language of the Book of Common Prayer* (London: Andre Deutsch. 1965), pp 192-219. The language of the Prayer Book, though beautiful has also been a barrier to providing adequate translation. Joshua Bloch, 'Early Hebrew Translation of the Book of Common Prayer', *Anglican Theological Review* 32:4. 1950. p 298 notes that Marianne Nevill's 1829 Hebrew translation of the Prayer Book for Jews failed on account of its attempt to convey too much of the original English form.

sought to emulate.[6] Whilst the people of God find their identity with the aid of the faithful of the past and indeed may hold themselves to account through the godly exemplars of the past, they do not need to copy the very details of their practice. Some things change and the historical difference of past and present ought not to be ignored.

We can learn from God's people of the past: what they wrote and how they encouraged each other and praised God when they met together – though this does not mean that we need to copy them. Thinking back to Hebrews, the use of history to help Christians understand their identity does not necessarily bind contemporary Christians to the interests and practices of the past. For example, as the author of the epistle interprets Psalm 95 in chapters 3-4, he makes it clear that the concern of the wilderness generation and the generation of Joshua was to enter the promised land. Yet for David, who wrote the psalm which promised rest to God's people and who was already living in the land, this was not a concern, nor should it be for Christians even though they do not have an earthly land to call their own. Likewise, in Hebrews 10:11-14, the priestly offerings in the temple through which God's people of the past related to Him are referred to, yet these are considered unnecessary for Christians who now have superior access to the same God through the Lord Jesus who 'by one sacrifice has rendered eternally perfect those who are being made holy.' There is no sense in Hebrews that the priestly offerings of the old covenant were bad in their own time, indeed, they served an important function fulfilling the requirements of the law (Hebrews 8:4), pointing forward typologically to a better sacrifice provided by the Lord Jesus (Hebrews 9:8-10) and reminding the people of God of the dreadful cost of forgiveness of sin (Hebrews 9:22, 10:3). But the priestly cult was appropriate only for a limited period of time, so the author of the Epistle argues in 9:10. Whilst the practice of God's people of the past may be a significant feature in his

---

[6] Cranmer's desire to emulate the practice of the early Church can be seen in his Preface (*Concerning the Service of the Church* in the 1662 Book of Common Prayer). Cranmer begins here by stating the reasons why the 'ancient Fathers' developed liturgy before arguing that subsequent liturgies represent a gradual departure from these ideals. 'But as these years passed, this godly and decent order of the ancient Fathers hath been so altered, broken, and neglected, by planting in certain Stories, and Legends, with multitude of Responds, Verses, vain Repetitions, and Synodicals'.

attempt to help his readers understand their identity as the people of God, the author of Hebrews does not give undue authority to the practices of the past. A central feature of his argument is that to trust in the efficacy of traditional temple worship is a failure of Christian discipleship: a failure to truly appreciate the significance of Jesus Christ. The past is addressed in a nuanced manner by the author of Hebrews, as something which can inspire as well as something which needs to be related to the present cautiously due to its potential to lead the people of God away from true faithfulness to Him.

2.2   *Anglican Identity and the Book of Common Prayer*

Of course, using liturgical practice to understand Anglican Identity is not an unusual enterprise, afterall, the Prayer Book is upheld as the official source of the Church of England's doctrine after Scripture in contemporary ordination services. Many recognise the appropriateness of the principle *lex orandi, lex credendi* (the word of prayer is the word of belief). Indeed, Rowan Williams argues that the quest for Anglican Identity needs to begin with a rigorous and sensitive observation of worship.[7] Yet Kenneth W. Stephenson highlighted the problem of attempting to define Anglican identity using the *Book of Common Prayer*, noting that the Prayer Book is a somewhat 'accidental' text that has been subject to considerable variation both prior to 1662, in terms of textual variation, as well as

---

[7]   Rowan Williams, 'Foreword to the Series,' in Ruth Meyers and Paul Gibson Ed., *Worship-Shaped Life: Liturgical Formation and the People of God* (Norwich: Canterbury Press. 2010), pp vii-xi. However, Williams would not see this as an historical observation but rather an observation of the present reality of Anglican worship. This may reflect Williams' debt to Continental Philosophy which tends to see identity as something established in the present moment, lacking a sense of diachronic fixity. Williams also maintains here, in an intellectual slight of hand, that the English Reformers themselves were keen to avoid any confessional fixity for the Church of England. This seems hard to maintain, given the Acts of Uniformity which established the exclusive use of the Book of Common Prayer.

after 1662 in terms of interpretation.[8] Despite this, the 1662 *Book of Common Prayer* has had something of a normative status within the Church of England for most of its history and bore a familial relationship to all other Anglican liturgies, at least until the 1970s. In the Church of England itself, the 1662 *Book of Common Prayer* was the principal 'official' liturgy until the introduction of *Common Worship* in 2000, since the *Alternative Service Book* defined itself as a supplement to, rather than a replacement of, the *Book of Common Prayer*.

In the introduction to Morning and Evening Prayer, Cranmer defines the purpose of the service as follows:

> And although we ought at all times humbly to acknowledge our sins before God; yet ought we most chiefly so to do, when we assemble and meet together to render thanks for the great benefits that we have received at his hands, to set forth his most worthy praise, to hear his most holy Word, and to ask those things which are requisite and necessary, as well for the body as the soul.

This definition forms the basis for the present study which looks out the nature and purpose of the Prayer Book Calendar, Collects, Lectionary and Psalter. These are features of the Prayer Book which define the year for Christians, guiding and feeding them through Scripture day by day and reminding them of all that God has done for them in the Gospel. It will be argued that these four features of the *Book of Common Prayer* urge Anglicans, or at the very least, members of the Church of England, to place the Bible at the centre of their Christian faith as they read, pray and remember day by day.

Evangelicals have often rejoiced in the scriptural doctrine of the *Book of Common Prayer* and, in times when they have found the

---

[8] Kenneth W. Stevenson, 'Anglican Identity: a chapter of accidents', in Kenneth W. Stevenson and Bryan D. Spinks Ed., *The Identity of Anglican Worship* (London: Mowbray. 1991), pp 185-191. Cf. idem., 'The Prayer Book as "Sacred Text"', in Charles Hefling and Cynthia Shattuck Ed., *The Book of Common Prayer: A Worldwide Survey* (Oxford: Oxford University Press. 2006), p 139 and Jeremy Gregory, 'The Prayer Book and the Parish Church: From the Restoration to the Oxford Movement,' in Charles Hefling and Cynthia Shattuck Ed., *The Book of Common Prayer: A Worldwide Survey* (Oxford: Oxford University Press. 2006), pp 93-105

Church of England most infuriating in its lack of commitment to such doctrine have found solace in the fact that at the heart of the Church is the *Book of Common Prayer.*[9] Indeed, at the same time, the *Book of Common Prayer* has been rejected by others for the Reformed character of its theology.[10]

Perhaps unsurprisingly, the focus of Evangelical interest has been the daily offices of Morning and Evening Prayer with their clear emphasis upon the severity of sin and the grandeur of grace, the order for the Lord's Supper and the debate over whether its theology is Zwinglian or Calvinist,[11] as well as the marvelous Articles of Religion. Yet the Prayer Book's framework of scriptural food and set prayers for the disciple of Jesus Christ also has much to teach us today. In the lectionary, with its aim for the Christian to read or hear the whole counsel of God each year, we see displayed an astonishing trust in the power of God's word to the change hearts and lives of those who are exposed to it. In the very simple calendar, we see both a great desire to celebrate the grand narrative of Christ's saving life,

---

[9] John Scrivener, 'Prayer Book Perspectives: Charles Simeon and the Prayer Book,' *Faith and Worship* 57. 2005. pp 41-46. The way J. C. Ryle, *Christian Leaders of the Eighteenth Century* (Edinburgh: Banner of Truth. 2002), p 117 describes the use of the Prayer Book by William Grimshaw, Perpetual Curate of Haworth is revealing, both for what it says about Grimshaw and the Evangelical Revival of the 18th Century, as well what it says about Ryle, an Evangelical in the 19th Century. 'The manner in which [Grimshaw] conducted public worship at Haworth seems to have been as remarkable as his preaching. There was a life, and fire, and reality, and earnestness about it, which made it seem a totally different thing from what it was in other churches. The Prayer Book seemed like a new book; and the reading-desk was almost as arresting to the congregation at the pulpit. Middleton, in his life of him, says: "In performance of divine service, and especially at the communion, he was at times like a man with his feet on earth and his soul in heaven...And his fervency often was such, and attended with such heartfelt and melting expressions, that scarcely a dry eye was to be seen in his numerous congregation."

[10] See, for example, the humorous invective by W. Jardine Grisbrooke, '1662 Book of Common Prayer: Its History and Character', *Studia Liturgica* 1:3. 1962. pp 146-166. Grisbrooke, writing about the second Edwardian Prayer Book, describes the Duke of Northumberland as 'one of the most violent and wicked men ever to hold high office in England'! (p 159).

[11] Gregory Dix, *The Shape of the Liturgy* (London: Dacre. 1945), pp 656ff. who also presents the case for Cranmer's Zwinglianism in this regard, though not an evangelical scholar. Cf. Richard Turnbull, *Anglican and Evangelical?* (London: Continuum. 2007), pp 9-97.

death and resurrection, as well as emphasis on everyday life seen in the vast expanse of Ordinary time, free from the interruption of special saints' days and festivals. In the Collects, we see something of the continuity of the Church of England with the best that was before it, as well as the importance of grounding our prayers in the steadfast character of God. The thorough use of the Psalter, read through each month, testifies to its value as material for prayer and praise, drawn from Scripture itself and engaging with the full variety of faithful living in a fallen world.

3. The Calendar: Rendering thanks for great benefits we have received at his hands

Liturgical and theological calendars are a fairly consistent feature of human religious systems generally, attempting to order the year in such a way as to involve certain times of remembrance or celebration or periods to pray for certain things, such as the harvest, emphasised in various forms of paganism. The Christian Calendars and, to some extent, the Jewish Calendars which preceded them are distinctively theological: they concentrate on reminding God's people year after year of the great events of salvation history. In the Jewish Calendar, which is based on the lunar cycle, significant periods are devoted to the exodus from Egypt (Passover), the giving of the law on Sinai (Pentecost), the day of atonement (Yom Kippur) and the successful Maccabean rebellion against Greek rule (Hanukkah). Whilst the origins of many of the features of contemporary Jewish Calendars are difficult to trace, it is clear from the New Testament and the Dead Sea Scrolls that many are very ancient indeed.[1] The Christian Calendars generally follow this historical focus, though all the historical events remembered relate to the ministry of Jesus Christ.[2] This is not surprising, since the earliest Christians, though they saw themselves as standing in continuity with the people of God before Christ,

---

[1] For example, significant events in the New Testament are linked with Jewish festivals. Indeed, the ministry of the Lord Jesus is well known to feature a yearly Passover in Jerusalem in John's Gospel. Likewise, 4Q318 of the Dead Sea Scrolls suggests something of the kind of Calendar to be much more clearly stated in rabbinic literature. Interestingly, and perhaps significantly, 4Q325 and 4Q321 depart from probable Jewish practice in antiquity by suggesting a solar calendar.

[2] Kenneth W. Stevenson, *Jerusalem Revisited: The Liturgical Meaning of Holy Week* (Washington: Pastoral Press. 1988).

recognised the ministry of Jesus as the climax of history: the most significant series of events ever to have taken place.[3]

It must be said that in many respects the Calendar in the *Book of Common Prayer* is very close to those which preceded it, such as the Sarum use. The two-fold division of the year into Advent to Trinity, focusing on the life and ministry of Jesus Christ, and Trinity to Advent, focusing on the demands of the Christian life, is the same. Likewise, the use of Collects relating to Epistle readings in Trinity follows previous use (with the exception of the Collect for the Second Sunday after Trinity which was composed for the 1662 Prayer Book). In addition to this, the grouping of fixed date Saints' days after the Trinity entries follows pre-Reformation practice.

Despite this similarity to older Western Calendars, something of an interest in Advent, Christmas, Passiontide and Easter can be detected through the sheer amount of minor revision of readings and Collects.[4] Perhaps the most significant development in the *Book of Common Prayer* is the creation of a special service for the Saturday before Easter with its own readings and Collect. This is important because previous calendars made no provision for this day, other than by means of the Easter vigil service, which is more of an anticipation of the day which follows it rather than a reflection upon Jesus' burial. Yet, even without the additions of the Prayer Book, the Calendar is significantly weighted towards these festivals and seasons, perhaps particular to Good Friday and Easter in terms of the amount of

---

[3]   Examples of this attitude in the New Testament abound. Hebrews 1:1-2 is a superb example ('At many times and in many ways, in the past God spoke to our fathers through the prophets [but] in these last days he has spoken to us through a son whom he has set as heir of all things and through whom he made the universe') as is 1 Peter 1:10-12 ('About this salvation, the prophets who prophesied the grace which is for you, searched carefully, carefully seeking for which time and circumstance the Spirit of Christ testified to beforehand: the Christ's sufferings and the glory after. It was revealed to them that they were serving not themselves but us who have now had announced to us – through those who have proclaimed the Gospel by the Holy Spirit send from heaven – those things which angels long to see').

[4]   These changes are described in some depth in Francis Proctor and Walter Howard Frere, *A New History of the Book of Common Prayer with a Rationale of its Offices* (London: MacMillan. 1910), pp 525-550. Prayer Book changes to Collects are discussed in some depth in the next chapter of this study.

Scripture appointed to be read, and, in relation to Good Friday, the number of Collects.

This focus upon the great events of Good Friday and Easter seems to reflect something of the theological emphasis behind the corporate meetings of the early Church. This emphasis can be seen in the interests of the apostolic kerygma witnessed in the speeches of the Acts of the Apostles and well as in practice of departing from meeting on the Jewish Sabbath to holding the 'Lord's day' as the day of resurrection. In the same way that the earliest Christians gathered to remember the saving events of the Lord Jesus' death and resurrection, so too the calendar of the *Book of Common Prayer* marks out these events as being of perhaps even greater significance than they had had in the medieval church. This focus on the climax of salvation history as something to be marked and celebrated at the heart of the Christian gathering is something worth imitating in contemporary Anglican worship.[5]

Whilst the Calendar in the *Book of Common Prayer* is heavily dependent upon earlier Calendars, it is also greatly simplified in comparison. This simplicity pertains particularly to the number of Saints days included within the Calendar. The *Book of Common Prayer* includes twenty-two fixed-date feast days for Saints throughout the year, including Holy Innocents and the Circumcision of Christ (Candlemass). In comparison the Sarum Calendar includes twenty for January alone. Whilst the Sarum Calendar includes a wide variety of Saints and Martyrs, the *Book of Common Prayer* Calendar includes only those people or events which are attested in Scripture. The medieval practice of the Western Church featured the use of both *Temporale* and *Sanctorale* Calendars. The 'Temporal' Calendar featured the seasons of the Christian year and principal feasts relating to events recorded in the New Testament. This aspect of the Calendar is retained in the *Book of Common Prayer*, though the use of different liturgical colours is removed in keeping with the Reformers' rejection of eucharistic vestments. The 'Sacred' Calendar featured a great number of saints days with special readings, post-communion prayers and collects. The *Book of Common Prayer* reduced the

---

[5]   James Palmer, 'Celebrating the Resurrection: A Theological Account of our Common Worship,' Churchman 122:1. 2008. pp 43-44.

'Sacred' Calendar to a simple list of 'black letter days': days which could be recognised if a minister wished to, but which lacked any special liturgical material to distinguish such days from any other.[6] This reflects the Reformers' interest in placing the Bible at the heart of the Calendar. It must be said that the saints days included in the 'Temporal' Calendar, which are thus included in the compulsory 'red letter days' of the *Book of Common Prayer*, are all people drawn from the New Testament. It is interesting to note that the proposed 1928 *Book of Common Prayer* attempted to promote pre-Reformation practice by supplying liturgical material for 'black letter days'.[7]

The Calendar of the *Book of Common Prayer* urges Anglican Christians to remember year after year the historical events through which they are set free from sin and granted entry into the Kingdom of God through faith in Jesus Christ. These events are foundational for a Christian's understanding of who he or she is. Without the regular, focused reminder of what it cost God to punish sin, Christians are in danger of forgetting just what an offence to God their sin is and are in danger of forgetting just how much they are loved by God. The Calendar is a reminder that Christians should not give up on remembering important events of the past on appointed days. Some days of the Calendar are regularly forgotten despite their immense theological importance, the most prominent example of which is Ascension Day. We may be tempted to give up on such days thinking that to recognise them is to declare them somehow more special or holy than others, or to regard them as essential. Such an approach is rigorously condemned in Col 2:16-17 and tends to force a separation between remembering the past and everyday life. But the past must be remembered if the Lord Jesus is to be followed faithfully. At the same time, Christians for whom the *Book of Common Prayer* is an authority should be wary of supplementing the Calendar with events or saints days which only relate in a secondary

---

[6]   Benjamin Gordon-Taylor, 'The Calendar,' in Paul Bradshaw, *A Companion to Common Worship*, Vol I (London: SPCK. 2001), p 41.

[7]   One of the suggested revisions of W. H. Frere was a return to the pre-Reformation ecclesiastical Calendar. See Ronald C. D. Jasper Ed., *Walter Howard Frere: His Correspondence on Liturgical Revision and Construction* (London: SPCK. 1954), p 24 and Gordon-Taylor, 'The Calendar,' p 41. Of course, this material has been supplied subsequently through the introduction of *Common Worship: Festivals*.

way to the events of the New Testament. If the events of Good Friday and Easter are celebrated within the same Calendar as lives of Christians from much later, such Christians of the past have their status elevated at the expense of the saving events of the Gospel.

In practice, any festival from the Calendar which enables Christians to proclaim the mighty deeds of God should be made the most of. This may mean embracing popular demand for festivals with greater enthusiasm as evangelistic opportunities as well as opportunities to remind the people of God of the great reasons they have for hope and rejoicing. It is beyond doubt that popular interest amongst the British public in special events, such as Christmas and Easter is steadily growing. This is evident in my own Church. Over a tenth of the population of the town attended a service on Christmas Eve in 2011 and our Easter Sunrise service regularly attracts over 400 people. Notable here is an interest in attending festival services which are somewhat unusual, such as attending the Lord's Supper at midnight or being up by 6.00 am with a bonfire. At the same time, other festivals, such as Ascension Day and Pentecost, attract significant public attention when they are observed in public with a certain element of theatre, such as the use of a rooftop choir. Evangelicals may shy away from some aspects of these festivals, particularly those with traditions that have possibly pagan origins (such as the Easter morning fire), yet these events provide opportunities to focus upon what God has done. Perhaps if Christians made more of celebrating Ascension Day, for example, they might have a better grasp of the Lord Jesus' heavenly reign, his priestly work and his future return, all of which are closely connected in the New Testament with the ascension.

4. The Collects: Asking for what is requisite and necessary

4.1 *The Collects of the Book of Common Prayer: Form and Content*

The Collects of the *Book of Common Prayer* are fine works or English prose. Yet, more than that, the Collects exemplify the confident character of Christian prayer, dependent upon the very nature and identity of God himself and the promises of his word. The origins of the term 'Collect' are somewhat ambiguous; reflecting both the collective nature of God's praying people as well as the nature of the prayer itself as collecting or summarising.[1] Cranmer appears to have employed both senses of the term and established the Collect as the only variable prayer in the Calendar.[2] In terms of the form of the Collect, matters are much more straightforward. A Collect is a single sentence prayer featuring a variety of traditional components as follows.

Invocation/Address

This is a vocative term addressing God to whom the prayer is addressed. Forms in the prayer book include 'Almighty God' (the most common), 'O Almighty God', 'O Lord God Almighty', 'Blessed Lord', 'O Lord', 'Lord', 'O God', 'God', 'O Lord God', 'Almighty and everlasting God', 'O everlasting God', 'Almighty and everliving God', 'Almighty and merciful God', 'Almighty Father', 'O God the King of glory', 'Lord of all power and might', 'merciful God' and 'O merciful God.

---

[1]   The latter being the principal meaning noted by Proctor and Frere, *History of the Book of Common Prayer*, p 523.

[2]   Toon, *Common Worship Considered*, pp 109-110. The particularly 'evangelical' aspect of the summarizing nature of the Collect is seen in instances in which the lectionary readings are referred to in the Collect associated with them.

Recital/Remembrance

In pre-Reformation liturgies including the Sarum Missal, the common form of address was Deus qui, featuring the relative pronoun to introduce a feature of God's character upon which the subsequent petition depends. In the *Book of Common Prayer*, the recital or remembrance often features a reference to one or both of the Scripture readings set for the day.[3]

Petition

Having addressed God and expressed something of his character, after a colon there follows the petition. This typically relates to the recital in some way and asks for something on behalf of the people of God.

Intention

The intention usually follows the petition and expresses a godly reason for making the petition, often taken from Scripture. The intention typically follows a semi-colon and begins 'that', then indicating what might result from the petition.

Pleading

The final clause of a Collect recalls the scriptural promise of mediation and access to God in the name of the Lord Jesus. The various forms include 'through him who liveth and reigneth with thee and the Holy Ghost, now and ever', 'through the satisfaction of thy Son our Lord', 'through Jesus Christ our Lord' (the most common), 'through thy son Jesus Christ our Lord' and 'grant this for thine only Son Jesus Christ's sake'. The pleading typically follows the intention after a semi-colon.

The Collect for the Circumcision of Christ might be regarded as a typical example of the Collect form.

---

[3] Toon, *Common Worship Considered*, p 111 notes that the recital in the Book of Common Prayer Collects is always in the second person, addressing God in prayer, rather than simply speaking to the people about God.

Invocation/Address:	Almighty God,
Recital/Remembrance:	who madest thy blessed Son to be circumcised, and obedient to the law for man:
Petition:	Grant us the true circumcision of the Spirit;
Intention:	that, our hearts, and all our members, being mortified from all worldly and carnal lusts, we may in all things obey thy blessed will;
Pleading:	through the same thy Son Jesus Christ our Lord.[4]

Whilst the short pleading of this collect is typical of the Prayer Book, Bridget Nicols and Peter Toon point out that, in contrast, *Common Worship* insists upon the use of the longer Trinitarian pleading: 'who is alive and reigns with you, in the unity of the Holy Spirit, one God, now and forever.'[5] The Prayer Book uses such pleadings only in the Collects set for major festivals. As those who regularly read or hear the Collects from *Common Worship*, the long pleading often seems unnecessary, even formulaic. In some collects this long pleading represents half of the text of the prayer.

It must be said that the majority of the collects in the *Book of Common Prayer* do not originate with Cranmer.[6] Many are ancient, translations of prayers found in the ancient Sacramentaries of Leo,

---

[4] Of course, there are many exceptions to this structure. The Collect for St Stephen's Day uses the vocative 'Jesus' in the intention. The Collect for the Fourth Sunday of Advent uses both a pleading and a doxology. See also the Collects for St John and the Third, Fourth and Fifth Sundays in Lent.

[5] Bridget Nichols, 'Collects and Post Communion Prayers', in Paul Bradshaw Ed., *A Companion to Common Worship, Vol I* (London: SPCK. 2001), pp 180-181 and Toon, *Common Worship Considered*, p 112

[6] Though Cranmer can be identified as the most prominent creative force behind the Book of Common Prayer. Grisbrooke, 'The 1662 Book of Common Prayer', p 146

Gelasius and Gregory.[7] This is by no means a fault, but represents the extent to which the *Book of Common Prayer* is a continuation of the liturgical traditions of Patristic Christianity and the extent to which the Church of England is part of the one Holy Catholic and Apostolic Church which God has built through the ages.[8] At the same time, the very act of translation into the vernacular speaks of the democratisation of Christian liturgy and Scripture desired by the Reformers. Cranmer wanted to see the liturgical treasures of the Ancient Church made available to anyone with ears to hear.

That Cranmer left many of the Latin Collects intact and in some cases made only minor changes is largely due to the doctrine contained within them. As James A. Devereux argues, in composing the 1549 and 1552 Prayer Books, Cranmer wished to create liturgy which proclaimed the utter fallenness of humankind, dead in its sin, and the necessity of God's grace. This desire was certainly behind Cranmer's work on the Collects. Yet Devereux notes that many of the Latin Collects which survived into the Sarum Breviary and which were available to Cranmer were distinctly Augustinian in tone, originating at a time when Pelagius had recently been condemned and sin and grace were understood in the same way that the Reformers were to understand them.[9] Because of this, many of the Latin Collects were not replaced nor indeed edited that much by Cranmer. Yet Devereux shows that in many cases where Latin Collects are adjusted by Cranmer the changes represent attempts to

---

[7] Charles Neil and J. M. Willoughby Ed., *The Tutorial Prayer Book* (London: Church Book Room Press. 1963), pp 149-150 note that five Collects are from Leo, twenty from Gelasius, twenty-seven from Gregory, one (the Collect for Easter Sunday) derived from both Gelasius and Gregory and one (the twenty-second Sunday after Trinity) from an Anglo-Saxon source. All of these Collects feature in the Sarum Breviary. The remaining Collects were composed and developed by the Reformers at various stages prior to 1662. These include most of the Collects for saints days, four Sunday Collects and the Collects for Christmas Day and Ash Wednesday.

[8] J. Todd Billings, 'The Catholic Calvin', *Pro Ecclesia* 20:2. 2011. pp 120-134 presents a similar assessment of Calvin's theology and its relation to Patristic and pre-Reformation theology.

[9] James A. Devereux, 'Reformed Doctrine in the Collects of the first Book of Common Prayer', *Harvard Theological Review* 58:1. 1965. pp 50-51. Cf. Samuel Leuenberger, 'Archbishop Cranmer's Immortal Bequest: The Book of Common Prayer of the Church of England: An Evangelistic Liturgy', *Churchman* 106:1. 1992. p 24.

emphasise the themes of utter sinfulness and the necessity of God's grace. For example, Cranmer deleted many uses of the term *mereamer* (to merit) since to 16th Century ears (though not to Patristic ears, Devereux suggests) it implied deserving good things from God through good works. Likewise, Cranmer added the word 'only' to the Collect for the Thirteenth Sunday after Trinity, so as to read,

> Almighty and merciful God, of whose only gift it cometh that thy faithful people do unto thee true and laudible service; Grant, we beseech thee, that we may so faithfully serve thee in this life, that we fail not finally to attain thy heavenly promises; through the merits of Jesus Christ our Lord.

It has been argued that such additions to the Latin Collects when translated in the Prayer Book are typically literary improvements as well. John Dowden argued that the Prayer Book Collects often contain more emotive language than the Latin originals.[10] Two examples of this, given by Dowden, are the addition of the phrase 'of thy tender love towards mankind' in the Collect for the Sunday next before Easter and the free translation of the phrase *bona invisibilia* in the Collect for the sixth Sunday after Trinity as 'such good things as pass man's understanding'.

In their early history, Collects were associated with the litany as summarising prayers, rather than the readings appointed to be read at the Mass in the Calendar. In the Sarum Breviary, the Collects, as in other late Medieval liturgies, are included alongside readings. Proctor and Frere point out that this association of the Collect with readings is enhanced in the *Book of Common Prayer* through the new reference certain collects make to the readings for the Lord's Supper, particularly the Epistle.[11] This can be seen most clearly in the first two Collects of Advent, both written for the 1549 *Book of Common Prayer.*

> Almighty God, give us grace that we may cast away the works of darkness, and put on the armour of light, now in the time of this mortal life, in which thy Son Jesus Christ came to visit us

---

[10] John Dowden, *The Workmanship of the Prayer in its Literary and Liturgical Aspects* (London: Methuen. 1899), pp 123-124. See also idem, 'Literary Aspects of Prayer Book Revision' *Contemporary Review* 18, Sept 1871. pp 267-283.

[11] Proctor and Frere, History of the Book of Common Prayer, p 525.

in great humility; that in the last day, when he shall come again in his glorious Majesty, to judge both the quick and the dead, we may rise to the life immortal; through him who liveth and reigneth with thee and the Holy Ghost, now and ever. Amen.

The structure of this Collect is unusual insofar as it lacks attribution of qualities to God but concentrates principally on the request and resultant clause. Nevertheless, it involves a characteristically Cranmerian relation to the Sunday readings which accompany it through direct reference to Romans 13. Likewise, the Collect for the Second Sunday of Advent,

> Blessed Lord, who hast caused all holy Scriptures to be written for our learning: Grant that we may in such wise hear them, read, mark, learn, and inwardly digest them, that by patience and comfort of thy holy Word, we may embrace and hold fast the blessed hope of everlasting life, which thou hast given us in our Saviour Jesus Christ. Amen.

This Collect derives both its recitation and intention from the Epistle associated with it: Romans 15:4-13. Yet it is not just Cranmer's 1549 and 1552 Collects which attempt to reflect the Bible readings to a greater extent than the Latin Collects. The Collect for the Third Sunday in Advent was probably written by John Cosin for the 1662 Prayer Book, replacing Cranmer's translation of the Collect from the Sarum Missal: 'Lord, we beseche thee, geue ear to our prayers, and by thy gracious visitation lighten the darkenesse of our hearte, by our Lorde Iesus Christe.'[12] Cosin replaced this prayer with the following:

> O Lord Jesu Christ, who at thy first coming didst send thy messenger to prepare thy way before thee; Grant that the ministers and stewards of thy mysteries may likewise so prepare and make ready thy way, by turning the hearts of the disobedient to the wisdom of the just, that at thy second coming to judge the world we may be found an acceptable

---

[12] The citation here is taken from the 1549 Prayer Book. The 1552 version retained this Collect with some minor adjustments of spelling. The Collect is a translation of 'Avrem tuam quesumus domine precibus nostris accomoda: et mentis nostre tenebras, gratia tue visitationis illustra.' Cosin's other Collects include that Easter Eve, the Third Sunday of Advent , the Sixth Sunday after Epiphany and the First Sunday after Easter.

people in thy sight, who livest and reignest with the Father
and the Holy Spirit, ever one God, world without end.

Cosin's Collect is superior to the translation of the Latin Collect in
several respects, despite the unusual address. The Latin Collect is
typically rather brief, reflecting the style of the short Trinity Collects,
lacking a recital. The recital 'who at thy first coming didst send thy
messenger to prepare thy way before thee' in Cosin's Collect enables
a more complex petition and intention by grounding these requests
in the character of God's mission of the past. The Latin Collect does
contain an allusion to the Epistle, 1 Corinthians 4:1-5. The phrase '*et
mentis nostre tenebras*' alludes to v.5 '*qui & illuminabit abscondita
tenebrarum*'. This allusion is rejected by Cosin, perhaps because of the
use of similar imagery in Cranmer's Collect for the first Sunday of
Advent, and two different allusions are used instead, one to the Epistle
and another to the Gospel (Matthew 11:2-10). The Gospel reading
provides the substance for Cosin's recital, particularly through its
reference to Malachi 3:1 in v.10. Yet, perhaps of greater significance is
that Cosin allows the Epistle to determine the nature of the petition,
since the Epistle's concern for the model of Christian ministry Paul
offers provides the basis for the Collect's prayer for 'ministers and
stewards' and the eschatological dimension to the Epistle is related in
the Collect. In the case of this Collect, one can see very clearly that
Scripture is seen to set the agenda for the Church's prayers.

Another significant difference between the Collects of the
Book of Common Prayer and those of earlier liturgies relates to the
Collects for saints days. The majority of Collects here are rewritten to
exclude the requests for intercession, made to the Saint, in pre-
Reformation Collects. As Proctor and Frere point out, the readings for
these days are not changed and the Collects instead pick up on some
quality of the Saint related in the readings.[13] The Collect for Saint

---

[13] Proctor and Frere, History of the Book of Common Prayer, p 550. F. E. Brightman, The
English Rite: Being a Synopsis of the Sources and Revisions of the Book of Common
Prayer with and Introduction and an Appendix, Volume 1 (London: Rivingtons. 1915), p
lxxiii usefully notes on the Latin saints' day Collects that 'in contrast with the usage of
the Orthodox East, invocation had comparatively little place in the ritual of the West. On
the other hand, 'comprecation' or prayers to God for the intercession of the saints, and
petition for a share in their merits, were general characteristics of prayers at
commemorations of saints.' This is the use of saints' intercession employed in the Latin
Collects for St Mark and St Matthias discussed below.

Mark's Day provides a clear example of this. The Latin Collect from the Sarum Breviary reads, '*Deus qui beatum Marcum euangelistam tuum, euangelice predicationis gratia sublimasti: tribue quesumus eius nos simper & erudition proficere: et oration defendi.*' The request for protection through St Mark's prayers in the final clause could not feature in a Reformed liturgy, such as the *Book of Common Prayer.* Hence, it is replaced as early as 1549 with a Collect which lacks this element. One aspect of the Latin Collect's petition is retained in Cranmer's recital which praises St Mark's teaching, through Cranmer's petition centres around an allusion to the Epistle (Ephesians 4:14). There is no obvious Scriptural allusion in the Latin Collect. Likewise, the Latin Collect for St Matthias reads, '*Deus qui beatum mathiam apostolorum tuorum collegio sociasti: tribue quesumus: vt eius interuentione tue circa nos pietatis simper viscera sentiamus.*' The notion of St Matthias' 'intervention' or 'intercession' is rejected by Cranmer who crafts his Collect around the Epistle from Acts 1:15-26, celebrating St Matthias' faithful apostleship and seeking the Church's preservation from false apostles (a probable allusion to Judas).

It must also be noted that the Collects' journey towards their final 1662 form also involved some revision of the original 16th Century translations, as well as replacements such as that mentioned above. Most of these revisions were minor, such as the introduction of 'O' for the vocative address in many Collects and the replacement of the personal pronoun 'which' with 'who'. When compared to its 1552 equivalent, the 1662 Collect for Saint John the Evangelist's Day could be said to contain a minor improvement. The use of the phrase 'walk in the light of thy truth' was added to the intention in the 1662 version and develops the light imagery of the pleading clause. This combination suggests the possibility of a conscious allusion to the light imagery used in the Johannine literature.[14]

---

[14] C. K. Barrett, *The Gospel According to St John: And Introduction with Commentary and Notes on the Greek Text* (London: SPCK. 1967), p 6 notes that whereas Matthew's Gospel uses the term φῶς seven times, as does Luke's, and Mark only once, the Gospel according to St John employs the term 23 times (33 in the entire Johannine literature). For studies in the use of this terminology in John's Gospel, see D. O. Via, 'Darkness, Christ and the Church in the Fourth Gospel,' *Scottish Journal of Theology* 14. 1961 and J. Dupont, 'Jésus-Christ: Lumière du Monde', *Essais sur la christologie de S. Jean* (Bruges: Éditions de l'Abbaye de Saint-André. 1951), pp 61-105.

4.2 *The Collects and Anglican Prayer*

Having seen something of the nature of the Collects in the *Book of Common Prayer*, how does this inheritance of prayer relate to Anglican identity and, in particular, Anglican prayer, today? Ramie Targoff argues that the Edwardian and Elizabethan emphasis on uniformity using the *Book of Common Prayer* had a primarily spiritual purpose, rejecting the traditional assumption that uniformity was merely concerned with achieving outward obedience without a care for an individual's personal faith.[15]

> This position stemmed not from a cynical indifference to the worshipper's inner state, but instead from an affirmative belief in what Aristotle describes as the efficacy of "habit." Hamlet's advice to Gertrude – "assume a virtue if you have it not" – originates from the behaviourist philosophy outlined in the *Nicomachean* Ethics, which posits a causal link between ethics (*ethike*) and habit (*ethos*). "Moral virtue," Aristotle declares, "comes about as a result of habit...For the things we have to learn before we can do them, we learn by doing them...we become just by doing just acts, temperate by doing temperate acts, brave by doing brave acts." This understanding of habitual practice helps to explain how the religious establishment could simultaneously seem uninterested in private belief and yet demonstrate repeatedly its desire to subsume private devotion within the public liturgy of the church. Indeed, what appears to be a simple request for an untaxing and potentially unmeaningful participation in a weekly service turns out to be a strategy to

---

[15] Ramie Targoff, *Common Prayer: The Language of Public Devotion in Early Modern England* (Chicago: University of Chicago Press. 2001), p 2 cites Patrick Collinson's observation that the famous 'quotation' from Elizabeth I about not wishing 'to make windows into men's soul' originates with Francis Bacon, not Elizabeth. See Patrick Collinson, 'The Elizabethan Church and the New Religion,' in Christopher Haigh Ed., *The Reign of Elizabeth* I (Basingstoke: Macmillan. 1984).

transform the worshipper's soul.[16]

According to Targoff, the liturgy of the *Book of Common Prayer* is meant to influence the faith or those who hear it. The *Book of Common Prayer* is a perfect example of the principle *lex orandi, lex credenda* (the law of prayer is the law of faith) forged by Cranmer to instil the Reformed faith in the people of England.[17] It is historically appropriate, then, to regard it as exemplary: as a liturgy which sets a standard for understanding God and how he should be approached. With this understanding, the Collects are not simply mindless regurgitation of older material, but are an expression of the kind of prayer and the kind of faith to be encouraged in faithful Christians of the Church of England. Since the Church of England has in no way unauthorised or disavowed the *Book of Common Prayer*, the Collects must be understood to set this example to the present day.[18]

Firstly, looking at issues of style, the Collects of the *Book of Common Prayer* are always addressed to God. The recitation, though it describes the nature of God and therefore informs those who hear the prayer, is still speech to God. In the same way the petition is directed to God and asks for definite and concrete things, such as the hearing of prayer or for an increase in godliness. The fact that such prayer addresses God so directly may seem obvious, yet there is a great deal which passes for prayer in contemporary churches which fails in this respect. Often a period of intercession may consist

---

[16] Targoff, *Common Prayer*, p 4. Targoff begins her study of religious language in 16th and 17th century England by analyzing various statements in Shakespeare's Hamlet which are indicative of an understanding that practice generates belief. The scene referred to in this citation is from scene two from act one. The reference to Aristotle's *Nicomachean Ethics* is to II. 1 and 5. Indeed, Aristotle posits not only a causal relationship between moral virtue and habit, but and etymological relationship too in II. 1, ἡ δ' ἠθικὴ ἐξ ἔθους περιγίνεταί ὅθεν καὶ τοὔνομα ἔσχηκε μικρὸν παρεγκλῖνον ἀπὸ τοῦ ἔθους.

[17] Devereux, 'Reformed Doctrine in the Collects', p 49

[18] Of course, the question as to the degree in which the early modern language of the Book of Common Prayer can be an agent in reforming Christian discipleship and developing trust in Jesus Christ today must be asked. For many, Prayer Book services represent an opportunity to disengage from the realities of everyday life. Mark Earey, 'Liturgical Formation and Education of the People of God,' in Ruth Meyers and Paul Gibson Ed., *Worship-Shaped Life: Liturgical Formation and the People of God* (Norwich: Canterbury Press. 2010), pp 48-49.

entirely of a list of things which are being prayed for. A prayer might run as follows,

> We pray for those who are poor,
> who are suffering,
> who are without food.
> We pray for those who are sick and those who are facing redundancy.
> Lord, in your mercy, hear our prayer.

Of course, it is right to pray for such things, but is the person leading these intercessions actually praying? Instead of directing petitions to God, this way of praying simply aims to suggest items for prayer to the people of God. The aim of praying in this way is possibly to enable individuals to make their own petitions. Or it may be that this style of prayer aims to avoid being restrictive by telling individuals exactly what to pray for. Or perhaps, this form of prayer is used to avoid controversy and the possible ethical or political views petitions might imply. For example, someone leading intercessions might be afraid of possible criticism for praying for help for those affected by government cuts (which could be seen as criticism of the government) or for the healing of broken families (which may be politically incorrect). It may, instead, be that this style of prayer reflects a lack of confidence in God's ability to answer prayer and hence asks nothing of him. If the Collects of the *Book of Common Prayer* represent exemplary prayer for the people of God, a faithful Anglican mode of prayer probably differs significantly from the practice of listing things to be prayed for in a time of intercession.

The Collects, since they are exemplary prayers, also model sound doctrine and, in particular, the human relation to the truths of the Gospel. Not only do they express God's character in their recitations, but they also express something of the appropriate human response to his character in their petitions and intentions. Therefore, John Richardson argues that the liturgy of the *Book of Common Prayer* represents an attempt by its principal author and redactor to communicate doctrine.

> The *Book of Common Prayer* is established on and seeks to impart the following understanding of the Christian gospel:
> That the chief issue between us and God is our sinfulness and his holiness.
> That we stand in constant need of Jesus's work of redemption

to deliver us from God's judgement and condemnation, and
That hearing the words of the Bible is fundamental to
establishing and maintaining our relationship with this
fearful and yet merciful God.'[19]

The Collect for Ascension Day is a good example of biblical doctrine,
stated clearly, setting the agenda for prayer. The prayer begins by
stating the fact of (thy only begotten Son) Jesus' ascension. The
petition itself cleverly uses the language of Colossians 3:1 to express
our need to set our hearts with the risen Christ now, in this life, and
also holds out the eschatological promise of life with the ascended
Lord. Richardson continues,

> The Church of England has long recognised the principle *lex
> orandi, lex credendi* – the law of prayer is the law of faith. The
> *Book of Common Prayer* was thus introduced not as an end
> in itself but as a means to an end, which was nothing less
> than the godliness of the people of God. Yet the Prayer Book
> also promoted doctrinal reform, and those who have since
> wanted to change the doctrines of the Church, from the
> Commonwealth, via 1928 to the present day, have likewise
> recognised the importance of liturgical revision.[20]

The Collects in the *Book of Common Prayer* present clearly the
identity of the God to whom Christians pray. The great benefit of this
is that it encourages our prayers to realistically reflect the character
and priorities of God, rather than simply praying selfishly or
unrealistically. This form of prayer is found repeatedly in the
Scriptures. For example, the petitions of Psalm 143:1-2 (to hear
David's prayer and to spare him from judgement) are predicated
upon two known facts about God's character (his faithfulness and his
hatred of sin).

> O YHWH hear my prayer, be attentive to my cry for
> compassion;

---

[19] John Richardson, 'Have we an Anchor? Reasserting the Doctrinal Role of the
Book of Common Prayer', *Faith and Worship* 68. 2011. P 12. Cf. Neil Patterson,
'How does Liturgy Articulate and Embody Doctrine?', *Faith and Worship* 65-66.
2010. pp 7-15 and Roger T. Beckwith, 'The Doctrinal Approach of the Reformers,'
Faith and Worship 65-66. 2010. pp 16-22.

[20] Richardson, 'Have we an Anchor?' p 16.

In your faithfulness and righteousness come to my aid.
Do not come into judgement with your servant;
For not one of all the living is counted as righteous before
you.

Unrealistic prayer might be that which ignores the promises of God.
For example, a Collect for miraculous healing (which is certainly a
good thing to ask for) may also be unrealistic since nowhere in
Scripture does God promise his people a pain free life, free from all
suffering: indeed, quite the opposite is promised! A Collect of this
sort would not be able to ground its petition in a recitation of God's
promises. The need to build petitions upon a reliable foundation of
an understanding of God's character and purposes is a sure antidote
to misguided prayer.

4.3   *The Prayer Book and Subsequent Collects*

The 1980 *Alternative Service Book* Collects are typically modernised
or modified versions of Prayer Book Collects. Such is the case with
the First, Second and Third Sundays of Advent.[21] At the same time,
many new Collects were introduced in 1980 which have no
antecedents in the Prayer Book, such as the Collects for the Fourth
Sunday of Advent and Christmas Eve. The latter is not even
recognised as a holy day in the *Book of Common Prayer.*

In the year 2000, many 'new' Collects were published in
Common Worship. Since then, a volume of shorter Collects has also
been published to accompany *Common Worship*, along with many
new Psalter Collects in the office book *Common Worship: Daily
Prayer.*[22] The Collects contained in *Common Worship* have much to
commend them. In particular, the reference made by many Collects

---

[21]   Though the Collect for the third Sunday of Advent in the ASB destroys the
allusion to 1 Corinthians 4 by changing the word 'mysteries' to 'truth', changes
the address to the more conventionally 'Almighty God' and generally 'dumbs
down' the incisive language of the Prayer Book Collect. For example, the phrase
'that at thy second coming to judge the world' is replaced by 'that when he comes
in glory'.

[22]   For a study of Psalter Collects, their structure and purpose, see Geoffrey
Grimshaw Willis, 'Curcus of the Psalter Collects', *Journal of Theological Studies*
21:2. 1970.

in the *Book of Common Prayer* to lectionary readings finds greater expression in *Common Worship*.[23] This is certainly a good development. However, the references to Scripture in the *Common Worship* Collects can often be unhelpful, perhaps skewing biblical interpretation towards reading people and events in Scripture as simply morally or spiritually exemplary. A good example of this form of biblical interpretation can be seen in the Collect for the Fourth Sunday of Advent, adapted from the Scottish *Book of Common Prayer*.[24]

> God our redeemer,
> who prepared the Blessed Virgin Mary to be the mother of your Son:
> grant that, as she looked for his coming as our saviour,
> so we may be ready to greet him
> when he comes again as our judge.

Here Mary is interpreted as an exemplar of patient waiting for the Lord Jesus. The very idea that Matthew or Luke intended to present Mary as exemplary in any sense is open to dispute.[25] Even if one does accept that Mary is presented as an exemplar to Christians, it is unlikely that the exemplary characteristic to be noted by readers is intended to be her expectation of a coming salvation. At no point is Mary described like Simeon as waiting for the coming 'consolation of Israel' (Luke 2:25). Whilst this Collect's interpretation of Mary is by no means heterodox, it does model a very shallow style of biblical interpretation in which the seasonal theme trumps the scriptural text. At the same time, it draws attention away from the distinctive ways in which the narratives about Mary advance what Matthew and Luke

---

[23] Although such reference to particular passages is often obscured by the Revised Common Lectionary and its use of years A, B and C, rather than a set of scriptural passages set to the same Collect each year.

[24] For the source history of this Collect, see Nichols, 'Collects and Post Communion Prayers,' p 184.

[25] Luke, who clearly presents his reasons for writing his Gospel in 1:1-4, suggests that his primary purpose is to present to truth about Jesus' life. The Gospels rarely hold up Jesus' family or followers as exemplary in any sense. Indeed, the use of Mark 3:31-35 which distances Jesus from his 'mother and brothers' in Matthew and Luke suggests that a special attention for the mother of Jesus is unlikely. Indeed, in the Matthean infancy narrative, the focus is on Joseph rather than Mary!

wish to proclaim about the coming of the Lord Jesus. In Luke, a Collect might do better to mention some of the astonishing claims Gabriel makes about Jesus to Mary in 1:30-33 or to note, as Mary herself does in the Magnificat, that in sending Jesus Christ, God is acting in his sovereignty to fulfil the promises he made to Abraham and his descendents for ever.[26] Likewise, a Collect for this Sunday might do better if it incorporated some of Matthew's emphases, such as the meaning of the name 'Jesus' and the profound description of him as 'Immanuel'.

The problem with praying using the text interpreted in this way is that the real challenge of the text is often missed and a shallow form of scriptural interpretation is encouraged. The Collects in *Common Worship*, unlike those in the Prayer Book, encourage Christians to look primarily for things in Scripture which address their experience and the problems they face. Of course, Bible reading and teaching should engage with the personal reality of living as a Christian. But Scripture speaks most powerfully when it is allowed to set the agenda, when reading attempts not to discover something easily and personally applicable, but when it attempts to hear the historically different, and perhaps strange, voice of the text. The habit of simply drawing examples from Scripture fails to do justice to biblical literature because it does not attempt to come to terms which the theological emphasis of particular texts. This is perhaps most pronounced in relation to the Gospels. In two of the Gospels a statement of the text's purpose is included to indicate why it has been

---

[26] The notion that in Christ God is fulfilling his (scriptural) promises of the past is a special theme of Luke's theology and is central in most attempts to define his approach to salvation history. See H. J. Cadbury, *The Making of Luke Acts* (New York: Macmillan. 1927), p 103, Hans Conzelmann, *The Theology of St Luke*, trans. Geoffrey Buswell (London: Faber and Faber. 1960), p 157, Helmut Flender, *St Luke: Theologian of Redemptive History*, trans. Ilse Fuller (London: SPCK. 1969), David Peterson, 'The Motif of Fulfillment in the Purpose of Luke-Acts', in Bruce W. Winter and Andrew D. Clarke Ed., *The Book of Acts in its First Century Setting, Vol I: Ancient Literary Setting* (Michigan: Eerdmans. 1993), pp 65-81 and Jacob Jervell, 'The Future of the Past: Luke's Vision of Salvation History and its Bearing upon his Writing of History,' in Ben Witherington Ed., *History, Literature and Society in the Book of Acts* (Cambridge: Cambridge University Press. 1996), pp 110-115.

written.[27] In each case, readers are informed that the particular Gospel has been written to tell them about Jesus Christ. This helps readers to see that they are told, for example, about the stilling of the storm, not to persuade them that the stilling of a storm is either possible or normal, but to show that Jesus is the Lord who reigns over the chaos of the wind and waves, the Lord who creates order out of disorder by a mere utterance.[28]

In addition to the Collects available in *Common Worship: Services and Prayers for the Church of England*, 2004 saw the publication of *Common Worship: Additional Collects*. The principal aim of this group of Collects is brevity. Take, for example, the Collect for the First Sunday of Advent.

> Almighty God,
> As your kingdom dawns,
> Turn us from the darkness of sin to the light of holiness,
> That we may be ready to meet you

---

[27] Luke 1:1-4 and John 20:30-31. For detailed analysis of the function of the former, see Loveday Alexander, *The Preface to Luke's Gospel: Literary Convention and Social Context in Luke 1:1-4 and Acts 1:1* (Cambridge: Cambridge University Press. 1993) and Michael Goulder, *Luke: A New Paradigm, Vol I* (Sheffield: Sheffield Academic Press. 1989), pp 199ff.

[28] It must be noted that the Prayer Book makes its own distinctive contribution to biblical hermeneutics: one worthy of greater scholarly attention given contemporary interest in attempt to define biblical hermeneutics with reference to Christian doctrine. Firstly, the important phrase from the daily offices 'the Scripture moveth us in sundry places' suggests an understanding of the text's agency upon the reader. This relates particularly well to Roland Barthes notion of the 'text of bliss' and Hans-Georg Gadamer's idea of interpretation as sharing the ontology of play. Article VII of the Articles of Religion asserts the essentially Christological focus of the whole of Scripture. This is certainly a theological hermeneutic which stands within the great 'pre-critical' traditions of interpretation. Yet, at the same time, the use of a Greek phrase in Article IX betrays the 'critical' and humanist origins of the reformers' approach to Scripture, in particular the quest to go *ad fontes*. Article XX bears a great deal of similarity to the Canonical interpretation made popular by Brevard Childs in the 1970s, since its demand that the Church 'may not so expound one place of Scripture that it be repugnant to another' indicates a belief that a consistent message runs through each book of the Bible. This is certainly a theological understanding of the Bible employing a strong sense of the text's divine inspiration.

In our Lord and Saviour, Jesus Christ.

Like the Prayer Book Collects, the Additional Collects avoid long Trinitarian doxological formulas or pleadings, except for special occasions, such as Christmas or Easter. This feature is certainly an improvement upon the Collects originally published in *Common Worship,* in which the Trinitarian formula certainly can sound formulaic, for want of a better word. However the quest for brevity in the Additional Collects typically succeeds at the expense of the recitation: the description of God's character which grounds the prayer in the nature, work and promises of God, so enabling the Christian to pray with confidence. Brevity can also make the Collect unclear. Take the Collect cited above, for example: what does 'as your kingdom dawns' refer to? Is the final clause a pleading or does it refer to meeting Christ spiritually, somehow, in the new season of Advent? Is the petition seeking a moral change or does it refer to the free status of holiness offered by Christ? However, it must be remembered that many of the Prayer Book Collects, particularly those of in ordinary time, are very short. Often this is also due to the reduction or exclusion of the recital, as is the case in the Collects for the Fifteenth to the Twenty Second Sunday after Trinity. This brevity was, amongst other reasons, a factor in prompting Puritan opposition to the Prayer Book.[29]

The Collects of the *Book of Common Prayer* offer Anglican Christians a wonderful model of what prayer ought to be like.

---

[29] Dowden, *Workmanship of the Prayer Book,* pp 120-121 notes that this was a particular target of the criticisms of Thomas Cartwright and the Savoy Conference and describes the apologetic responses of Richard Hooker, Henry Hammond and Jeremy Taylor, defending the brevity of the prayers in the Prayer Book. Cf. Neil and Willoughby, *Tutorial Prayer Book,* p 151. It must be noted, rather sadly perhaps, that William of Orange (following the advice of the Dean of Canterbury, John Tillotson) sought a revision of the Prayer Book in 1689 which might have gone some way towards reconciling non-conformist Puritans to the liturgy of the Established Church. However, the drafted 'Liturgy of Comprehension' was never even discussed at Convocation and failed to be authorized for use in the Church of England. See Timothy J. Fawcett, *The Liturgy of Comprehension 1689: An Abortive Attempt to Revise the Book of Common Prayer* (Southend-on-Sea: Mayhew-McCrimmon. 1973). Interestingly, as well as lengthening many of the Collects from the 1662 Book of Common Prayer, the Liturgy of Comprehension also introduced a greater amount of reference to the lectionary readings associated with the Collects within the Collects themselves.

According to this model, Anglican prayer ought to be firmly rooted in the Scriptures, based on the character and promises of God. Anglican prayer ought to embody a realism, based on a biblical understanding of God, of what it is right and proper to ask of God. At the same time, prayer ought to seek God's will by intending God's glory and human submission to his purposes. Because this prayer is based upon the character and purposes of God, it can be prayed with confidence. Anglican prayer should also have an eye to the instruction and edification of other Christians, relating, like the Collects, the great doctrinal truths of the Gospel.

Churches which do not read a Collect in their meetings might consider using them as model prayers and, in sympathy with their earliest purpose, as summarising prayers. The Collects of the *Book of Common Prayer* are certainly the best authorised Collects to be used. If the archaic language of these is Collects is perceived to be a barrier to comprehension, an 'unauthorised' modernisation of them exists in the *English Prayer Book*, available through the Church Society website.[30]

---

[30] http://www.churchsociety.org/publications/englishprayerbook/index.asp

5. The Lectionary: Hearing his most holy Word

A Lectionary is simply a systematic programme of Bible reading. Lectionaries have existed for much of Christian history, following traditions set by Rabbinic Judaism. There is evidence of both one and three year programmes in which the whole of the Old Testament is read within these time periods. There is also some evidence to suggest that when the Lord Jesus himself preaches from a lectionary reading as he takes up the scroll of the Prophet Isaiah in Luke 4:16-21.[1] One of the most tantalising possible glimpses of the lectionary in the New Testament comes from the sermons in Acts which appear to follow the form of much later (rabbinic) synagogue sermons, preaching on each set text for the day and relating them to each other.[2] This suggests that the earliest Christians might have made use of lectionaries akin to those witnessed much later. Cranmer sets the scene for the Lectionary of the *Book of Common Prayer* in the Preface to the 1549 Book, preserved later as the essay, 'Concerning the Service of the Church', describing Medieval practice.

> When any Book of the Bible was begun, after three or four Chapters were read out, all the rest were unread. And in this sort the Book of *Isaiah* was begun in *Advent*, and the Book of *Genesis* in *Septuagesima*; but they were only begun, and never read through: After like sort were other Books of holy Scripture used. And moreover, whereas Saint *Paul* would have such language spoken to the people in the Church, as

---

[1]   Though this remains a matter of uncertainty since the most compelling references to the use of lectionaries are much later than the time of Jesus' ministry and, indeed, the lastest possible dating of Luke. Alfred Plummer, *A Critical and Exegetical Commentary on the Gospel According to S. Luke* (Edinburgh: T & T Clark. 1898), p 120 notes that Jesus is not recorded as having asked for the Isaiah scroll, it being simple handed to him, suggesting that it was a predetermined text for the day. Likewise, both Plummer and Howard Marshall, *The Gospel of Luke: A Commentary on the Greek Text* (Carlisle: Paternoster and Grand Rapids: Eerdmans. 1978), p 182 note that the verb εὑρεν (he found) does not imply that Jesus found the passage at random. Interestingly, the earliest extant testimony to the use of Lectionaries comes from *b. Tal. Meg.* 32a, the text of which is very late but probably represents earlier traditions.

[2]   J. W. Bowker, 'Speeches in Acts: A Study in Proem and Yelammedenu Form,' *New Testament Studies* 14:1. 1967.

they might understand, and have profit by hearing the same; The Service in this Church of *England* these many years hath been read in Latin to the people, which they understand not; so that they have heard with their ears only, and their heart, spirit, and mind, have not been edified thereby.

Three things are particularly distinctive in the Lectionary of the *Book of Common Prayer* when compared with the lectionaries which preceded it: the exclusive use of biblical and apocryphal texts and the aim to read the whole of the Canon each year. Pre-Reformation Lectionaries featured a wide variety of material, some scriptural, some the writings of saints and church fathers and some legendary or hagiographical. Against this background, the Prayer Book Lectionary offers a clear expression of the Reformers' belief in the sufficiency of Holy Scripture detailed in Article VI of the Articles of Religion. Henry Chadwick argues that the inclusion of the apocrypha within the lectionary suggests something of a middle way between the full inclusion of such texts in the Lutheran lectionaries and the radical Reformation and Reformed tendency toward their total exclusion.[3] Furthermore, Chadwick notes that texts from the apocrypha are referred to on a number of occasions in the first book of Homilies, suggesting that Cranmer and his associates gave significant weight to the apocrypha.[4] However, when one takes Article VI of the Articles of Religion into account, a much more Reformed account of the apocrypha is suggested, though one which falls far short of that in the Westminster Confession. Article VI draws a sharp distinction between canonical books of the Bible and 'other Books' which may be edifying but which should not provide exclusive grounds for points of doctrine. However, this distinction does not appear to have influenced the lectionary.

Apart from extensive use of the Psalter, pre-Reformation Lectionaries did not attempt to relate the whole of Scripture on a regular basis. Again, the more thorough approach taken in the

---

[3]   Henry Chadwick, 'The Context of Faith and Theology in Anglicanism', in Arthur A. Vogel Ed., *Theology in Anglicanism* (Wilton: Morehouse Barlow. 1984), p 16.

[4]   Examples include; Misery of all Mankind, Judith 4 and 9, Wisdom 7, Baruch 2; Christian Faith, Ecclesiasticus 1, 15, 32 and 44; Swearing and Perjury, Ecclesiasticus 23; Falling from God, Ecclesiasticus 10, Fear of Death, Ecclesiasticus 41, Wisdom 3 and 4.

Lectionary of the *Book of Common Prayer* testifies to the Reformers' belief in the importance of the public reading of Scripture.[5] Each year, the Old Testament was to be read in its entirety once, the New Testament three times and the Psalter twelve times. Not only was Scripture to be read thoroughly, it was to be read in the vernacular. To understand why, one must return again to Cranmer's 1549 preface.

> There was never any thing by the wit of man so well devised, or so sure established, which in continuance of time hath not been corrupted: As, among other things, it may plainly appear by the Common Prayers in the Church, commonly called Divine Service. The first original and ground whereof if a man would search out by the ancient Fathers, he shall find, that the same was not ordained but of a good purpose, and for a great advancement of godliness. For they so ordered the matter, that all the whole Bible (or the greatest part thereof) should be read over once every year; intending thereby, that the Clergy, and especially such as were Ministers in the congregation, should (by often reading, and meditation in God's word) be stirred up to godliness themselves, and be more able to exhort others by wholesome doctrine, and to confute them that were adversaries to the truth; and further, that the people (by daily hearing of holy Scripture read in the Church) might continually profit more and more in the knowledge of God, and be the more inflamed with the love of his true Religion.

---

[5] The public reading of Scripture is well attested as an early Christian practice. See, for example 1 Timothy 4:13, 'until I come, be devoted to public reading of Scripture (πρόσεχε τῇ ἀναγνώσει), to exhortation and to teaching'. The Greek term used here does not automatically imply the 'public' nature of the activity, but when one examines how it is used in 1 Esdras 9:48 and Nehemiah 8:8 this element is obvious. Public reading of Scripture as a feature of synagogue worship which appears to have been continued by the early Christians (see Luke 4:16, Acts 15:21 and 2 Corinthians 3:14). One of the earliest 'Jewish' witnesses to this practice is the Qumran text 1QS 6:7-8. Cf. Josephus, *Ant.* 11:123. Christian writings also appear to have been read publically from a very early date (Colossians 4:16, 1 Thessalonians 5:27 and Revelation 1:3). In later Christian practice, public reading of Scripture was often performed by a designated and practiced *lector*, see Tertullian, *De Praescriptione Haereticorum*, 41 which is the first mention of such an office, apparently adopted from Catholic Christianity by the heretics Tertullian condemns.

Matthew Williams points out that Cranmer's desire to make Christians as familiar as possible with the Bible was nuanced by his appropriate concern to ensure that biblical interpretation remain within the confines of apostolic orthodoxy.

> The vernacular Bible was intended to unleash the power of God's word in bringing people to a sound mind and genuine faith, not to introduce a sort of doctrinal individualism. To that end Cranmer introduced two more instruments of reform: vernacular common prayer and prescribed vernacular homilies. These would cause people to recite and hear sound doctrine at every service of worship, thus guiding them into a correctly balanced understanding of Scripture.

> Indeed the whole principle of common prayer is a natural extension of this concern ... It was not enough to pump the people full of Scripture, one had to guide what they affirmed in response to Scripture with prayers, creeds and other affirmations of the whole counsel of Scripture. Common prayer was Cranmer's strategy to rein in 'contentious disputing'.[6]

In this respect, it must be noted that the *Book of Common Prayer* belongs firmly within the world of Magisterial Reformation. Just as Zwingli fought with the Anabaptists in Zurich and Calvin sought to quell the influence of Severatus and the Libertines in Geneva, so Cranmer's passion for placing the Bible in the hands and hearts of ordinary Christians is coupled with a passion for the objective truth witnessed to in the Bible. Because of this, Cranmer secured the interpretation of Scripture by keeping the liturgy as the context in which Scripture is primarily heard.[7]

However, Cranmer's ambitious aim to saturate the Church with Scripture was not to last. In 1871, a revised lectionary was introduced which reduced the amount of Scripture read at Morning and Evening Prayer so that the New Testament was read only twice a year and the apocrypha read even less than in the earlier lectionary.

---

[6] Matthew Williams, 'Read Aloud for Power, Read Together for Doctrine: The English Reformed Theology of the Bible,' *Churchman* 124:2. 2010. p 148

[7] Richardson, 'Have we an Anchor?', pp 9-10.

Today, if a lectionary is used at all in the Church of England, it is typically the *Common Worship* Lectionary, inspired by the ecumenical Revised Common Lectionary.

The *Common Worship* Lectionary has much to commend it as well as several significant flaws when compared to the Lectionary in the *Book of Common Prayer*. Firstly, the prescription of shorter and fewer passages can be an aid to the serious exposition of Scripture, since it is much easier both for the preacher and the congregation to engage with a more focused set of readings. The adverse of this is obviously that less Scripture is read, which may be seen simply as a loss. Certainly, the *Common Worship* Lectionary provides less of a challenge to Christians who only hear lectionary readings of a Sunday, since Sunday readings are typically from familiar passages. The proposed 'Pillar Lectionary' exemplifies this flaw by defining certain readings as essential, a canon within the canon, and by abandoning entirely the systematic exploration of Scripture. Such an approach has been widely criticised for its failure to expose Christians to the whole counsel of God, presenting instead something of a sanitized or safe version of the Bible.

So what challenge does the *Book of Common Prayer* Lectionary have for Anglican identity today? J. I. Packer asks,

> Why ... do we not soak ourselves in Scripture, as our Prayer Book Lectionary asks us to? From the amount of Scripture set to be read each day of the year it is plain that our Reformers meant the Anglican Church to become the greatest Bible-reading church in Christendom, and Anglican Christians to become the most knowledgeable Bible students to be found anywhere.[8]

Are Anglicans 'the most knowledgeable Bible students to be found anywhere?' It is doubtful. The Prayer Book Lectionary places to reading of Scripture right at the heart of the Christian life, day by day. Anglican Christians are to spend serious amounts of time exposed to the word of God. And not just to the seemingly 'safe' and familiar passages, rather the whole counsel of God. This is quite a challenge to

---

[8]   James I. Packer, 'For Truth, Unity, and Hope: Revaluating the Book of Common Prayer', *Churchman* 114:2. 2000. p 105.

us today when our devotional Bible reading may feature a passage of some 20 verses or even fewer. This is a challenge to our services which avoid long readings from the Bible and which often choose readings from a very limited pool. It can be a sadly revealing exercise to search for sermon recordings on the websites of churches with a long-established tradition of faithful expository preaching. Often there are whole books of the Bible which have barely been heard in the 20 years since recording began. Often, out of 30 talks on, for example, Luke's Gospel, 20 will be on familiar passages such as the infancy narratives preached at Christmas services. Anglican Christians ought to follow the example laid out in the Lectionary of the *Book of Common Prayer* and seek to spend more time learning from God's word.

Rather sadly, the Revised Common Lectionary is unable to help in this regard. Since the majority of Anglican Christians who make Church attendance a priority probably only attend once a week, they are only likely to be exposed to a limited selection of famous passages on a three year cycle. These passages are usually not 'difficult' ones, likely to encourage Christians to think through controversial subjects, nor do they necessarily follow each other: there are often significant gaps and leaping from book to book. Indeed, it is unlikely, given the reality of weekly Church attendance, that the observance of a lectionary would serve Cranmer's aim of seeing the Church of England exposed to the whole of God's word. Churches which read through whole books from one week to another are more likely to reflect this aim, but only if they ensure that their reading follows a long-term programme which aims to include the whole Bible over time.

6. The Psalter: Setting forth his most worthy praise

In 1530, George Joye published an English translation of Martin Bucer's new Latin version of the Psalter. According to G. J. Cumming, this event represents the first liturgical expression of the English Reformation.[1] Whilst this event was no doubt radical, the liturgical use of the Psalter is an extraordinarily consistent feature of the worship of God's people, both before and since Christ. When Christians today praise and pray using the Psalter they stand within a great tradition. It has been generally accepted since the work of Sigmund Mowinckel that the Psalms played a significant role in the temple worship of ancient Israel.[2] Whilst some of his suggestions for the *Sitz im Leben* of particular psalms employ unwarranted speculation, many of Mowinckel's suggestions are fairly clear from the texts themselves, and, in particular, from their superscriptions. The liturgical use of the Psalter in the early Church appears to be evidence in the writings of the New Testament. At the very least, it is clear that certain psalms were well known by first century Christians, particularly Psalms 2, 8, 16, 33, 110 and 118. Likewise, the use of the Psalter both in private devotion as well as public liturgy is well attested in the Patristic period and beyond.[3]

The Psalter of the *Book of Common Prayer* was taken from the 1539 Great Bible, largely the fruit of Miles Coverdale's scholarship (influenced by the work of Joye), though the Psalter in the Prayer

---

[1] G. J. Cumming, *A History of Anglican Liturgy* (London: MacMillan. 1969), p 49. Interestingly, the phrase 'saving health' (a very odd translation of a quite common term usually rendered 'salvation') in Psalm 67:2 in both the Book of Common Prayer and the Authorised Version is likely to have originated with Joye.

[2] Sigmund Mowinckel, *The Psalms in Israel's Worship, Vols I and II*, trans. D. R. Ap-Thomas (Oxford: Oxford University Press. 1967). Cf. Walter Brueggemann, *Worship in Ancient Israel: An Essential Guide* (Nashville: Abingdon Press. 2005), pp 22-23, 33-34 and 41ff.

[3] See, for example, Tertullian, *De Oratione* 27, Athanasius, *Letter to Marcellinus* and Augustine, *Retractiones* 2.11. Anthony Gelston, *The Psalms in Christian Worship: Patristic Precedent and Anglican Practice* (Norwich: Hymns Ancient and Modern. 2008), p 17.

Book does not agree precisely with any extant versions of the Great Bible.[4] A detailed study of the style and accuracy of Coverdale's translation of the Psalter can be found in Dowden's, *The Workmanship of the Prayer Book*.[5] Suffice it to say that the translation is far from perfect, though many of its defects are due to a desire to create something of greater poetic value for easy liturgical use. Cranmer's 1549 preface describes sporadic the use of the Psalter in the Medieval Church.

> And furthermore, notwithstanding that the ancient Fathers have divided the *Psalms* into seven Portions, whereof every one was called a *Nocturn*. Now of late time a few of them have been daily said, and the rest utterly omitted.

Cranmer's aim, in contrast, was to promote a *recitatio continua* (continuous recitation) of the Psalter, enabling it to be read in its entirety each month. The 1549 *Book of Common Prayer* had adaptations to allow for different numbers of days in the month in the recitation of the Psalter. However, the 1662 Prayer Book allowed for the Psalter not to be read in its entirety in February. The instruction 'the Order how the Psalter is appointed to be read' in 1549 reads,

> To every Month, as concerning this purpose, shall be appointed just xxx days. And because January and March hath one day above the said number, and February, which is placed between them both, hath only xxviii days, February shall borrow of either of the Months (of January and March), one day, and so the Psalter, which shall be read in February, must begin on the last day of January, and end the first day of March.

Whereas the instruction in the 1662 *Book of Common Prayer* reads,

> The Psalter shall be read through once every Month, as it is

---

[4] Brook, *Language of the Book of Common Prayer*, pp 148-149. Often these variants are the result of printers' comparisons of the Prayer Book Psalter with other versions, the occasional misreading of words and letters as well as the replacement of archaic words with more contemporary words. An example of the latter, given by Brook, it the replacement of 'mowes' (mouths) with 'grimaces' in Psalm 35:15 in the 1662 version.

[5] Dowden, *Workmanship of the Prayer Book*, pp 175-191.

there appointed, both for Morning and Evening Prayer. But in February it shall be read only to the twenty-eighth or twenty-ninth day of the Month.

Because of Cranmer's desire to see the Psalter read once a month, the number of psalms read or sung at Morning or Evening Prayer tends towards three to five, depending on the size of the psalm. For many Christians, this is rather an onerous requirement, one which can make the recital of the psalms rather tiresome. In 1872, the parliamentary 'Act for the Amendment of the Acts of Uniformity' permitted clergy to use just one psalm at Morning and Evening Prayer or one stanza of Psalm 119 if on the twenty-fourth to the twenty-sixth day of the month. This modification certainly has much to commend it to contemporary use of the Prayer Book Psalter, especially outside of a cathedral or college chapel context in which a gifted choir may be able to lead the singing of several psalms set to a variety of chants, beautifully. It could be argued that, whilst it is no doubt laudable to expose the people of God to as much of the word of God as possible, limitations of attention and receptivity make it more practical (and, perhaps, more edifying) to employ only a single psalm. Yet the great difficulty with this approach is that it forces a minister to choose which psalm to use. Invariably, a minister will choose one which quite short and not too challenging.

The proposed 1928 *Book of Common Prayer* bracketed certain parts of the Psalms for optional omission as 'unedifying'. Mercifully, this practice is not included in *Common Worship*, though the concern prevails.[6] Just as Christians benefit from being exposed to the full and challenging diversity of Scripture in the Prayer Book Lectionary, the exhaustive reading of the Psalter is similarly challenging, presenting readers with real difficulties, such as the psalmist's desire to see Babylonian children killed in Psalm 137:9. At the same time, the breadth of expression in the Psalter might provide something of a counterweight to the often bland triumphalism of recent Christian music and other liturgical material. Terry J. Wright argues that the full use of the Psalter enables a much more realistic

---

[6] However, Jane Sinclair, 'The Psalter,' in Paul Bradshaw Ed., *A Companion to Common Worship, Vol I* (London: SPCK. 2001), p 241 seems to suggest that the division of some psalms into paragraphs in *Common Worship* may be intended to separate parts of a psalm which may be deemed 'difficult' by some.

expression of human feelings to God in worship. Wright notes the extent to which psalms such as Psalm 88, which offers no sense of hope or comfort, are utterly alien to the very limited range of feelings much contemporary liturgy and music expresses.[7] Christian meetings which make liturgical use of the whole Psalter may in fact give expression to much more of the Christian experience, especially those aspects of the Christian life which are most painful and difficult. This argument is also made by Anne Harrison, who recommends practical ways of including more of the Psalter in Sunday services as well as resources which set the Psalms to music other than Anglican Chant.[8]

Yet the tradition of *recitatio continua* has broadly been rejected since the introduction of *Common Worship*. *Common Worship: Daily Prayer* emphasizes choice in the use of the Psalter. Under the heading 'Choosing the Psalmody' it recommends the use of the psalm cycles from *Common Worship* weekday lectionary and well as its own seasonal cycles. In this volume, the service of Prayer During the Day provides two cycles, one lasting a month and another lasting a fortnight, progressing through Psalm 119 and the Psalms of Ascent.[9] Andrew Mein, writing as an Old Testament scholar, notes that a principal argument used by opponents of the practice of *recitatio continua* is a perception that the Psalter is a collection of liturgical texts, rather like a hymn book. It is argued that since few Christian gatherings would sing through a hymn book in this way,

---

[7] Terry J. Wright, 'The Darkness of Isolaton: Suffering Worship'. An unpublished paper used by special permission. Dr Wright is an Associate Research Fellow at Spurgeon's College whose blog is at http://christpantokrator.blogspot.com.

[8] Anne Harrison, *Recovering the Lord's Song: Getting Sung Scripture Back into Worship* (Cambridge: Grove Books. 2009), particularly pp 4-6 and 11-21. Cf. Martin Kitchen, 'The Bible in Worship', in Kenneth W. Stevenson and Bryan D. Spinks Ed., *The Identity of Anglican Worship* (London: Mowbray. 1991), pp 41-42 who recommends thematic groupings of the Psalms rather than the simple monthly journey from the beginning to the end of the Psalter laid out in the *Book of Common Prayer*.

[9] *Common Worship: Daily Prayer* (London: Church House Publishing. 2005), pp xi and 24. Cf. *Celebrating Common Prayer: A Version of the Daily Office SFF* (London: Mowbray. 1992), pp 688-689. This volume, which exercised a significant influence over the development of *Common Worship: Daily Prayer*, also includes seasonal psalm collections which to not employ the whole of the Psalter within the year. Yet, in addition to this, it includes a table of Psalms with which the whole Psalter can be read every seven weeks.

from start to finish, there is little reason to take this approach with the Psalter. But Mein argues that this view of the Psalter as a simple collection does not take account of recent research in Biblical Studies which highlights the extent to which the Psalter is structured as a whole.[10] A feature of this more recent research (and, in fact, it is only as recent as the work of Brevard S. Childs in the 1970s), for example, is the suggestion that Psalm 1 (and possibly 2 and 3) serves as an introduction to the Psalter, indicating that it is intended to be understood as a composite whole.[11]

The sense in which the Psalter gives expression to the full range of experience in the Christian life must be held in tension with the way in which the Psalter witnesses to Christ. Peter Toon argues that the *Book of Common Prayer* urges Christians to read the Psalter Christologically, just as it was read and understood prior to the Reformation.[12] Whilst there is nothing within the liturgy of the *Book of Common Prayer* to suggest this, Article VII of the XXXIX Articles of Religion states that,

> The Old Testament is not contrary to the New: for both in the Old and New Testament everlasting life is offered to Mankind by Christ, who is the only Mediator between God and Man, being both God and Man. Wherefore they are not to be heard, which feign that the old Fathers did look only for transitory promises.

However, it is unclear whether the Psalter in *Common Worship* is intended to be read Christologically. Here, the second translation of Psalm 8:5, which broadly follows that of the New Revised Standard Version, makes such Christological reading difficult. Here the psalm reads 'what are mortals, that you should be mindful of them; mere human beings that you should seek them out?' The Hebrew term *anōsh* in the first clause possibly has the universal and gender-neutral sense implied in the term 'mortals', though it is usually applied to a

---

[10] Andrew Mein, 'The Daily Office and the Shape of the Psalter', *Studia Liturgica* 33:2. 2003. pp 240-243.

[11] Brevard S. Childs, *Introduction to the Old Testament as Scripture* (London: SCM. 1979), p.513 and more recently, Samuel Terrien, *The Psalms: Strophic Structure and Theological Commentary* (Grand Rapids: Eerdmans. 2003), p 75.

[12] Toon, *Common Worship*, p 126.

singular male, but the translation of *ben adam* as 'mere human beings' (whilst also potentially gender-neutral) is problematic because it destroys the ambiguity of the referent of what is traditionally translated 'Son of Man.' This singular, eschatological, as well as gender-exclusive term is noticed by the author of the Epistle to the Hebrews who employs the term to refer to the Lord Jesus, who as the Son of Man is made lower than the angels for a brief period through the incarnation, before being crowned with glory and honour. Christians of the Church of England should be reluctant to diverge from the widespread practice of seeing Christ in all the Scriptures, especially as they pray and praise using the Psalter.

Cranmer's prescription of *recitatio continua* is another example of his aim to place the Bible at the heart of the Church of England. In addition to the great benefit of enabling Anglicans to have these texts of Scripture written on their hearts, this practice also enables Anglican services to represent to full scope of real, everyday life witnessed in the Psalter. Anglican services are not simply to offer a serene escape from the day to day struggles of Christian discipleship. The continuous use of the Psalter ensures that difficult feelings, such as those of the psalmist in Psalm 88, are expressed to God and not swept under a carpet of respectable self-righteousness. Whilst it may be difficult to keep to Cranmer's program of readings from the Psalter, and, indeed, one could rightly argue that there is no reason why the Psalter, amongst all the books of the Bible, should be the only one to be read twelve times each year, it is no doubt valuable to make more of this liturgical resource.

7. Conclusion

The Anglican tradition has, over the centuries, clearly been affected by a variety of influences. At different times and periods in its history differing weight has been attached to these emphases. We are unwise to dismiss or exclude those that give currency to particular strands of the tradition. However, it is also the case that there is a core identity of Anglicanism which lies in the Protestant Reformation settlement and the particular emphasis, understanding of Church and ministry, doctrine and practice which that embodies. Variety on both sides has indeed been part of the richness of Anglicanism, but we should be careful not to invest such variety with a weight of interpretation that it cannot bear.[1]

It must be said that for the majority of the Church of England's history, assuming that that history begins with the Royal Supremacy under Henry VIII, one liturgy has predominated. That liturgy is the 1662 *Book of Common Prayer*, itself only a minor modification of its 1552 and 1559 predecessors. The Prayer Book is probably the most important text for exploring the identity of the Church of England and consequently Anglicanism more generally. This liturgy stands within the mainstream of Reformed theology, reflecting the concern of the reformers to place the Bible at the heart of the life of the Church, day by day, as well as their concern to stand in some continuity with the ancient Church, both apostolic and patristic. These concerns are seen in the way the Calendar emphasizes the biblical events of the cross and resurrection of the Lord Jesus. They are seen in the way that the Collects replicate the best of the Collects of previous liturgies whilst enhancing the use of biblical allusion in Collects generally and purging them of elements which contradict Reformed theology, such as the petition of the saints. Furthermore, these Reformed concerns are displayed by the lectionary's aim to expose Christians to the whole council of God each year and by the thorough and methodical use of the Psalter the Prayer Book suggests. As Turnbull argues, at the heart of the Anglican tradition is a very clear statement of Reformed concerns, the

---

[1]   Turnbull, *Anglican and Evangelical?* p 46.

acceptance of which has been the defining mark of belonging to the Church of England for most of its history. No other feature of Anglican history can come close to matching the significance of the *Book of Common Prayer.*

Latimer Publications

LATIMER PUBLICATIONS

LATIMER PUBLICATIONS

LATIMER BRIEFINGS

LB01	The Church of England: What it is, and what it stands for	R. T. Beckwith
LB02	Praying with Understanding: Explanations of Words and Passages in the Book of Common Prayer	R. T. Beckwith
LB03	The Failure of the Church of England? The Church, the Nation and the Anglican Communion	A. Pollard
LB04	Towards a Heritage Renewed	H.R.M. Craig
LB05	Christ's Gospel to the Nations: The Heart & Mind of Evangelicalism Past, Present & Future	Peter Jensen
LB06	Passion for the Gospel: Hugh Latimer (1485–1555) Then and Now. A commemorative lecture to mark the 450th anniversary of his martyrdom in Oxford	A. McGrath
LB07	Truth and Unity in Christian Fellowship	Michael Nazir-Ali
LB08	Unworthy Ministers: Donatism and Discipline Today	Mark Burkill
LB09	Witnessing to Western Muslims: A Worldview Approach to Sharing Faith	Richard Shumack
LB10	Scarf or Stole at Ordination? A Plea for the Evangelical Conscience	Andrew Atherstone
LB11	How to Write a Theology Essay	Michael P. Jensen

LATIMER BOOKS

GGC	God, Gays and the Church: Human Sexuality and Experience in Christian Thinking	eds. Lisa Nolland, Chris Sugden, Sarah Finch
WTL	The Way, the Truth and the Life: Theological Resources for a Pilgrimage to a Global Anglican Future	eds. Vinay Samuel, Chris Sugden, Sarah Finch
AEID	Anglican Evangelical Identity – Yesterday and Today	J.I.Packer, N.T.Wright
IB	The Anglican Evangelical Doctrine of Infant Baptism	John Stott, Alec Motyer
BF	Being Faithful: The Shape of Historic Anglicanism Today	Theological Resource Group of GAFCON
TPG	The True Profession of the Gospel: Augustus Toplady and Reclaiming our Reformed Foundations	Lee Gatiss
SG	Shadow Gospel: Rowan Williams and the Anglican Communion Crisis	Charles Raven
TTB	Translating the Bible: From Willliam Tyndale to King James	Gerald Bray
PWS	Pilgrims, Warriors, and Servants: Puritan Wisdom for Today's Church	ed. Lee Gatiss
PPA	Preachers, Pastors, and Ambassadors: Puritan Wisdom for Today's Church	ed. Lee Gatiss
CWP	The Church, Women Bishops and Provision: The Integrity of Orthodox Objections to the Proposed Legislation Allowing Women Bishops	

ANGLICAN FOUNDATIONS SERIES

FWC	The Faith We Confess: An Exposition of the 39 Articles	Gerald Bray
AF02	The 'Very Pure Word of God': The Book of Common Prayer as a Model of Biblical Liturgy	Peter Adam
AF03	Dearly Beloved: Building God's People Through Morning and Evening Prayer	Mark Burkill
AF04	Day By Day: The Rhythm of the Bible in the Book of Common Prayer	Benjamin Sargent

Lightning Source UK Ltd.
Milton Keynes UK
UKOW051013180812

197737UK00001B/21/P